# Throug Eyes

*Thoughts Sentiments & Memories*

by
## Belinda Conniss

The poems in this book are sentiments and memories written by me, unless otherwise stated. I have also included a couple of poems by friends which have special meaning to them. I have credited those poems with their name and an explanation.

# In Memory

My Father, Thomas Black McGinty
25.10.1935 – 25.02.1992
Sadly, I didn't get to meet you.
But without you I wouldn't have existed.

My Daughter Rosie 26,12,1998
Forever loved and in my heart.

My Mother-In-Law, Rosanna Canning (McCool)
17.01.1945 - 17.07.2004

# Dedication

This book of poems is, in part, in dedication to loved ones who are no longer with me, also to the mothers and children of *Tuam in Galway* and *Sean Ross Abbey in Roscrea, Co Tipperary* and all mother and baby homes that continue to pull heavy on my hearts.

# Contents

Our Rose In Heaven

Rose Garden

Angel Calling

Music To My Ears

Sounds Of The Shore

I Was Just A Child

I Said No

That Gun

Time For Change

Long Winding Road

Look In The Mirror

You're Not The One

On The Road Again

I Should Have Known

Yes, I Loved You

Hurt

You Ran

My Time To Shine

No Different

Homeless

Did You Know?

Bitter

Lost Without My Child

Friendship

Don't Look Down

Penny Caramel

Room Fourteen

A Scot's Hogmanay

I'm Not Only A Tree

Time

A Childs Love

Parents

Our Home

Those Were The Days

Silence

Today We Said Goodbye

Country Road

They'll Keep On Fighting

# Preface

As a teenager I discovered that I could very often recite poetry but having lack of confidence I never spoke of it and although in school we would recite poetry of the likes of Robert Burns I was never very confident in standing up in front of everyone, fast forward a little over thirty years and I'm writing poetry and enjoying it.

# Introduction

My first two books, *Sad, Lonely & A Long Way From Home* and *Secrets & Lies* were autobiographical, published in 2016.

I then went on to write my first book of poetry *Tears On My Pillow,* followed by my first fictional book *The Empty Swing,* published in 2017. Also published in 2017 *Where Water Flows & Grass Grows.* In *Through My Eyes* I have amalgamated both books previously published to include new poetry written to date. In this book you will find the stories through my thoughts as well as dedications and sentiments in memory of family & friends no longer with me, some of which may relate to others.

If you would like to keep informed about the release dates of future books and much more, then please follow me on my website www.insideoutlastyle.com.

*Belinda Corliss*

*'Finding the words to explain difficult and traumatic experiences can bring relief, it's the beginning of the healing process and the end of a dark chapter in one's life'*

# You Never Saw Those Tears I Cried

*'Many of us cry in secret, rarely letting others see those tears.'*

Some people can totally fake it. They can smile and laugh; they can act like everyone else, even while they are in excruciating emotional pain.

Faking it is easy, it doesn't matter who you are we all have that mask we wear that stops unwanted questions when we would rather not discuss the things that get us down.

We can smile and laugh even when we would rather curl up in a corner and have nobody bother us.

We try to act like nothing is wrong, but it's hard and we know when we do it people must notice the difference, whether it be our body language or the way in which we talk.

It doesn't matter how much pain we are suffering or how hard we try to hide it, we are just kidding ourselves because everyone can see it, some are just too afraid to ask what is wrong for fear of upsetting us.

# Tears On My Pillow

*'If you cannot see the tears in my eyes,*
*Surely, you must feel the pain in my heart.*

There is no shame in crying,
We must let those tears flow,
Never hold on to that pain,
Just let those tears go.

They say the prettiest smiles,
Hide the deepest secrets,
The prettiest eyes have,
Cried the most tears.

They say the kindest hearts,
Have felt the most pain,
I've cried so many tears,
I have none left, not a grain.

The hardest tears to wipe away,
Are those that are invisible,
There's pain and hurt in my heart,
I'm certainly not invincible.

There are tears on my pillow,
Whenever I lay my head,
When you are out of sight,
And I lay in my bed.

So sit for a moment,
And try to understand,
The pain you have caused,
With your heavy hand.

# When I'm Gone

When I'm gone the tears will flow,
But there is something that you should know,
The love I have for all of you,
You don't really have a clue.

Too busy putting me down,
Makes me feel like a clown,
I've done so well in my life,
But you just cut me with a knife.

You did not appreciate the things I've done,
Nor did you treat me like a loved one,
Hidden secrets you kept from me,
Didn't you realise one day I would see?

How could you be so blind
To all I had to offer?
Me, friend, sister and daughter,
Sometimes I felt like a squatter.

So now I'm gone you're shedding tears,
Something you should have done through the years,
Now I've gone it is too late,
My words you will remember, on this date.


I find it easy to forgive,
In peace go on make sure you live,
One thing I want you to hear,
Don't let my memory disappear.

# Do Not Bully Me

They say ignore the bullies they're only jealous of you,
How do they know that when work is all they do?

Tears roll down my face when I'm alone at night,
Don't they realise I try with all my might?

They call me names, they say I'm to blame,
I can't help how I look, I'm not looking for fame.

They bully me when I'm in school,
They know they're breaking the rules.

I can't take it anymore what should I do?
I could end it all because of you.

But then a thought comes to mind,
They have a broken home, how could I be so blind.

Just maybe, maybe they're alone,
Someone to talk to in their own zone.

Understanding is all they need,
A friend like me a friend indeed.

*(Written for those who may have suffered, or are suffering, bullying.)*

*'For nothing is hidden that will not manifest, nor is there anything secret that will not be known and come to light.'*

~ Luke 8:17

# Father's Day Again

Its Father's Day again,
My thoughts turn to you,
Wishing you were here with me,
But then, what could I do?

They didn't tell me that you existed,
Until it was too late,
Now every Father's Day,
My heart will always ache.

I have your picture in my hand,
Trying to imagine,
The life we could have had,
If they had taken action

They say that the eyes,
Are the windows to the soul,
If you could look inside mine now,
My heart you could console.

So with heavy heart,

I listen to my song,

And say my prayer to God,

Please, don't make this day too long.

*In Loving Memory of my Father:*
*25.10.1935 – 25.02.1992*

*Song: 'My Father's Eyes' By Eric Clapton*

# Siblings

They say that you're my brothers,
But how can this be so?
I've heard little about you,
And never any show.

I don't have a photo,
That lets me see your face,
I can only look at our father,
And imagine you that way.

I didn't get the chance,
To meet our dad at all,
I hope it's not the same for us,
Please don't make me crawl.

One brother I have met,
Another two to go,
I'd like to get to meet you,
Or would you even show?

The brother that I've met,
Is the oldest of us all,
He knows not much of you,
So this has to be your call.

# Me To You

Forever I will miss you,
Forever I will cry,
Why did you have to leave me?
And gain your wings to fly.

We didn't get the chance,
To spend some time together,
That's why I will miss you,
Always and forever.

*(Author unknown, I have incorporated some of my own words to this poem)*

# Daddy Can You Hear Me?

You missed all my smiles, you missed all my tears,
You missed all my laughs, you missed all my fears,
I hope you come find me and see who I've become,
You can come and see me when my day will come.

Do you ever think of me, do you ever wonder?
Do you know that I'm scared of lightning and thunder?
Have you forgotten who I really am?
Well, I'm the baby girl you and Mum never planned.

Did you ever love me, did you even care?
Would you have held me like a teddy bear?
Do you have a picture that you hold in your hand?
Or are you too scared to know who I am?

Well, I'm your little girl, the one you didn't plan,
When you found out they say that you ran,
I hope to get to know you when my day will come,
'Cause daddy can you hear me? In blood we are one.

*(Author unknown, I have incorporated some of my own words to this poem.)*

# Always My Father But Never My Dad

I'm sorry you missed out when I went to school
for the first time,
And you didn't have me tell you that you were all mine.
I'm sorry that you weren't there to take me to the mall,
And you weren't there to tell me I have to stand tall.
Sorry you weren't the one I saw when
I came home that day,
Or the one I would run to when I had a bad day.
Sorry you weren't there to tell me there is nothing to fear,
But, then again, you should have been there.

I'm sorry you weren't the one to teach me to ride a bike,
Or the one who took me on my first ride.
I'm sorry you weren't the one who carried
me on his back,
Or the one who held me tight when strength was
what I lacked,
I'm sorry you weren't the one to hold me when I cried
Or tell me I did great when I really tried.
I'm sorry you weren't there to teach me how to cook,
Or here at night to read me my favourite book.

I'm sorry that you never had me in your life at all,
But I forgive you, Father, rather than to fall.
It broke my heart when they told me that you

already passed,
And knowing that you looked for me was a bigger blast.
I know now that you loved me and wanted me
in your life,
But then again, you had another wife.
So, father be proud of me and all I have become,
Until we meet that day when our hearts will be one.

*(Author unknown, I have incorporated some of my own words to this poem.)*

# Why We Hold On To Memories?

*'I take a walk down memory lane, because it makes me smile and it eases my pain.'*

How many times have we said that we have had enough and wanted to pack our bags and run? I know I have many times in the past.

However, I never did, back then I didn't drive so it was easier to just go for a long walk.

A long walk; keep walking until I find somewhere quiet and peaceful just to gather my thoughts and recharge the batteries.

# Our Mother

Behind her shadow,
I stand tall,
It was a tough battle,
Her pain and all.

An ocean of tears,
Behind her smile,
Tormented, trapped and torn,
Her heart was always worn.

All those years,
Her heart wouldn't heal,
I know she is looking down on us,
With love and pride she'll feel.

Knowing that I've found you,
You, her little boy,
Her heart now,
Full of Joy

Now we are together,
Brother's that we are,
Always and forever,
Never again to part.

*(Written for my Husband to his brother)*

# Our Rose In Heaven

Fourteen years today since God called you home,
Not a whimper, not a moan,
He didn't warn us it was his plan,
For he knew we wouldn't understand.

God needed you, his special Rose,
Where you'll blossom and continue to grow,
Now in heaven many roses there are,
They've grown from you wide and far.

Now heaven has the sweetest scent,
It's what God wanted, love well spent,
Heaven now filled with roses,
So many colours and beautiful poses.

Now we know why God took you home,
His love for you he's always owned,
We feel your presence, smell your scent,
When God sends you home for a day to spend.

Know that we miss you; think of you every day,
We would not have it any other way.

Like heaven, we fill our home with roses too,
Cause only God knows how much we love and miss you.

*In Loving Memory of my Mother-in-Law Rose (Rosie)*

# Rose Garden

I planted a rose bush in memory of you,
Each side of my door and in full view.

Each summer they come into full bloom,
The smell lingers right into my room.

I planted more in each corner of the garden,
With a sleeping angel to guard them.

Red and white roses, there are so many,
I wouldn't change it not for a penny.

I ask God to protect you each time in my prayers,
As I lay here at night with silent tears.

Those roses they're never far from my touch,
Always remember, we love you so much.

*In Loving Memory of my Daughter, Rosie*
*(26.12.1998)*

# Angel Calling

I see their faces in the clouds,
Oh! I wonder, I say out loud,
Is it me or is it real?
Is this how they make us feel?
They say they leave a calling card,
But it's just a feather in the yard.

The smell of scent you recognise,
But can't remember their demise,
Then it hits you out of the blue,
A loved one looking out for you,
Is it real, is it true?
Could this be their way to you?

A sudden noise that you hear,
Could it be that they are near?
A sudden breeze in one spot,
Can explain such a lot,
Is it real, is it true?
They are, indeed, with you.

Feather, smell, noise,
We'll never know if it's true,
But comfort, indeed, it'll bring to you.

*'It takes a minute to find that special person, an hour to appreciate them and a day to love them, but it takes an entire lifetime to forget them.'*

~ Author unknown

# Music To My Ears

Here's that song again,
The one that makes me cry,
With many happy memories,
Of days that have gone by.

There's a story to be told,
In every song that's sung,
Of all the happy times,
You and I were one.

Although you are in heaven,
In music you are here,
Your memory lives on,
In thoughts held so dear.

# Sounds Of The Shore

Listening to the waves upon the evening shore,
Brings back a flood of memories,
Once buried deep down to the core.

We look up to the sky and wonder,
If you're watching us sat here,
Knowing that we love you with memories so dear.

Your life was short, that we know,
There was nothing we could do,
God had other plans, that's why he chose you.

We know you're always by our side,
We often hear your call,
We hear those little knocks on our bedroom wall.

In our heart you'll always stay,
We wouldn't have it any other way,
So know that we know you're always there,
Loved very dearly and we'll always care.

*'The scars from mental and physical abuse can be as deep and long lasting as the punches and slaps.'*

~ Author unknown

# I Was Just A Child

I stood there crying when you touched me that night,
I was so scared, I just couldn't fight,
I was eight-years-old, you were eighteen,
Did you think that you were supreme?

I was just a child you knew that it was wrong,
I couldn't scream out, you were so strong,
I cried in bed at night unable to tell,
Scared if I told that they would yell.

I moved away it, stopped for a while,
We moved far away, more than a mile,
Sometime after, you came back to stay,
My heart was pounding on that day.

By now I was fourteen-years-old,
But that didn't stop you, you were so bold,
You kept saying those nasty things,
It disgusted me right through to my limbs.

You moved away when I wouldn't succumb,
But the things that happened could not be undone,
It's sad when I think someone else may be suffering,

Are others safe while you're shuffling?

I can't help thinking can you do any worse?
Are you even able to show some remorse?
I'd like to think that those filthy thoughts,
Touched no other child you came across.

# I Said No

Another row that made me jump,
And yet again, another thump,
You only had to lift your hand,
And every time I would jump.

Looking back everyone was right,
You were a coward no man would you fight,
Why I let you do it I will never know,
One thing for sure, I suffered with every blow.

I cried when you took me that night,
I had no strength, I could not fight,
I told you no but you carried on,
I think you thought I was just some hoe.

You were such a brute, you used such force,
You never did show any remorse,
But God saw it happen, he has plans for you,
And trust me he will see them through.

# That Gun

Your gun was loaded when you shoved it in my face,
You were rabbit hunting as you did on a daily basis,
Would you really have pulled the trigger?
Bringing shame to your family, well, go figure.

You said you would throw acid in my face,
If you thought another man would take your place,
Why did you say the things that you said?
What was really going on inside your head?

You even told me how to wear my hair,
As you looked at me with such a snare,
I wore it up, you wanted it down,
You made me look like a clown.

I suffered in silence before I knew what to do,
Your manipulation was right on cue,
"Enough," I said, "or you'll drive me away."
After which you made me pay.

You didn't like if I spoke to a man,
I've got news for you, I will if I can,
You controlled me for far too long,
I found my strength, and now I'm gone.

*'If your dreams don't scare you, they aren't big enough'*

~ Author unknown

# Time For Change

Sitting here every day,
Wondering why as I pray,
Many years I worked so hard,
Not now I'm pretty scarred.

What shall I do to pass the time?
I ask myself, always a whine,
A service for others that's what I'll do,
Baskets and flowers but to name a few.

Then I decided to write my book,
And, trust me, it was no notebook,
Twenty years it's taken me to write,
The future is now looking bright.

Now I'm writing another, the sequel,
But it's not like Eddie the Eagle,
Writing the first was the best thing I've done,
It has given me a taste, I've almost won.

Now I know I've nothing to prove,
You cannot look at me and disapprove,
I've always known I'm strong enough,
But not you, who took the huff.

# Long Winding Road

It was a long road driving through the glens,
Not a straight road, mind, so many bends,
Hills as far as the eyes could see,
Oh, such beauty, this is definitely for me.

Many years I've dreamt of this,
A cottage in the hills, oh, such bliss,
One of these days my dream will come true,
Sat there thinking of you.

Coal fire burning on a cold winter's night,
Snow falling heavy, all pure and white,
What I would give to have this in my life,
Sat in my cottage, no trouble, no strife.

# Look In The Mirror

Those wrinkles I see, they are not mine,
Staring in the mirror not looking so fine,
Who is this woman? I do not know,
Oh, she looks like she's taken a blow.

In my heart I know it's me,
But my head does disagree,
Look at this tired old face,
Give yourself a shake, you're a disgrace.

Off to the salon to have my hair done,
Then to the nail bar, now I must run,
Off to the mall to buy some new clothes,
Now I'm not feeling quite so coarse.

Back home I'm looking glam,
Feeling much better, I am,
Looking in the mirror no more an old face,
Someone sophisticated has taken my place.

Now I'm feeling on top of the world,
As I watch in the mirror taking a twirl,
Make more of an effort I tell myself,
You're not ready to be left on that shelf.

*'The emotion that can break your heart is sometimes the very one that heals it.'*

~ Nicholas Sparks

# You're Not The One

You're not the one to tell me what I can and cannot do,
What made you think I'd come running back to you?
This life I live is full of many places,
So I'll take my time and fill those empty spaces.

You said you wanted freedom from the love
that we shared,
So I packed my bags that's just how much I cared,
You're feeling lost without me,
Please, don't call anymore, just let it be.

I have no time for you anymore, as you let me go,
Too much time has gone by, go find some other beau,
I've now moved on with my life, another man
has caught my eye,
So please just let me go, its time to say goodbye.

I know now that you're feeling much regret,
The past is in the past, please try to forget,
It will help you to move on,
If you now think of me as gone.

# On The Road Again

I've travelled this road so many times,
Hundreds of miles to get to mine,
The road is long, not many bends,
When will it stop, when will it end?

I've seen so much along the way,
Not many people know where I stay,
Alone with my thoughts, daydreaming and all,
Soon I must stop to visit the mall.

Food shopping for one is never much fun,
As lonely as I am, it's only one bun,
No one to love, no one to stray,
No one to hurt me, I'd rather it that way.

# I Should Have Known

What made you think I could trust you after this?
You did your best but it was anything but bliss,
We did have some wonderful years,
But some of those brought nothing but tears.

Those tears I cried were not of joy,
Looking back, you were just a boy,
Those women you had, were just your toys,
Shame you didn't act like the big boys.

I should have known better,
Why ever did I read that letter?
The shock made my heart pound,
Knowing you were sleeping around.

Did you know how you made me feel?
Did you realise my heart would never heal?
Now you're the one with the broken heart,
Everyone thought I played a part.

Now they know I was not at fault,
You were the one that brought it to a halt,
You should have known better,
Cause, now me, I'm the jet-setter.

# Yes, I Loved You

Back then I gave you my all,
And you thought you'd never fall.

But that wasn't enough, you wanted more,
So you took and took till you hit the floor.

I was young and naïve, I found it hard to believe,
The man that I loved could so easily deceive.

As the years went on, things got harder,
Your lies and deceit no longer mattered.

Why you did it I do not know,
One thing's for sure, you've nothing to show.

Now I'm happy and in love, the man I married,
Is more than enough, no more tears and nothing to fear.

What have you got to show for it all?
Another broken marriage and more kids to manage.

I wished you well when you fell,
Finding a wife who will complete your life.

# Hurt

It hurt me when you told me,
You no longer cared,
Like a little girl,
I ran scared.

What was I to you?
For the years that I had given,
Just so you know,
I have forgiven.

I won't forget,
The wrong that you have done,
You broke my heart,
How could I forget that part?

Now you have nothing and no one.
And, yes, it is all real.
Now you know how you made me feel.

# You Ran

Thinking of you and the times that we had,
Where did they go, they weren't all bad?
But you wanted more I couldn't provide,
So you ran to her, a place you could hide.

You said you were low and needed someone,
Someone who understood you, who you'd become,
I wasn't enough, you wanted more,
Truth is, I became a bore.

Why did you think she was the one?
To give to you when I had none,
I gave it my all but it wasn't enough,
You wanted us both, she was your rough.

You married her and had kids,
What a shock it was, back to bibs,
Like me, she wasn't enough in the end,
She, too, drove you round the bend.

Then you found yourself a much younger lady,
I'm beginning to think your head's a little hazy,
You're getting old now, nowhere to run,
You've had so many ladies, they see you come.

You're now on your own with no one to blame,
With your conquests you brought nothing but shame,
So the moral of the story I have to say,
Your life now is looking rather grey.

*'Never allow others drama or hate stop you from being you.'*

~ Author unknown

# My Time To Shine

Many years I've waited for the day,
That you will see me in a different way,
You said I was no good,
Always put me in a mood.

Who were you to even say?
She'll not go far every day,
Watching now, I see you stare,
Say it now, if you dare.

I've travelled far and wide,
Worked so hard to provide,
I started at the bottom, worked to the top,
And, even then, you would not stop.

Me; that girl you said wouldn't go far,
And, yes, believe me, I still carry that scar,
Tell me what have you achieved?
Through all the years you disbelieved.

I've taken a punch or two, yes, even from you,
Was I hated that much or was it a grudge?
Never there when I needed you,
Never a hug, you didn't have a clue.

Looking back, I see it now,
Your insecurities while raising your brow,
Looking down with your envy,
Those looks you give, ever so deadly.

Now I'm older I have not changed,
But your attitude is so deranged,
When will you ever learn?
It does not pay to be so stern.

# No Difference

There is no difference between black and white,
So why all the conflict? Give up the fight,
You took their land, that wasn't very bright,
They didn't invite you there so what gave you that right?

You employ them as servants in their homeland,
They cannot live freely, so much having been banned,
You wonder why they have a chip on their shoulder,
I mean, really, can you be any colder?

I pray for the day that we can be one,
So do me a favour and put down your gun,
Don't walk around in a stupor,
Let's make the change for a better future.

# Homeless

See me sitting here,
Looking for help,
From those so dear.

Passers-by keep on walking,
Just a glance, no one talking.

Yes, I have a pet,
Something I don't regret.

Disapproval from your eyes,
Why is that no surprise?

I do without to feed my pet,
My only friend, no regrets.

"Get a job," I hear you whisper,
I had it all, please don't whimper.

The day may come,
You lose it all.

Trust me, it's not your call.

# Did You Know?

Did you know when I had my first kiss?
I was thirteen-years-old, but he kissed like a fish,
A kiss I'm sure never to miss.

Did you know the first song that I loved?
It was Adam and the Ants, 'Dog Eat Dog',
Now I'm pretty sure he wouldn't have kissed like a frog.

Did you know the first book that I read?
It was Mills and Boon, a love story I'd read,
Thinking back, I was so easily led.

Did you know the first job that I had?
In a shoe shop, it wasn't all bad,
Shoes galore in such a small store.

Did you know the first love of my life?
I was almost his wife, maybe it was me,
One thing is for sure, it wasn't to be.

Did you know the first time that I travelled?
Majorca I went, I was so dazzled,
The sun was so hot I almost frazzled.

Did you know the first marriage I had?

It ended in tears but was not all bad,
It was the one thing that made me sad.

So now you know a little more about me,
What do you think?
What do you see?

*(One of the hardest things in life is realising that not even family know the real you.)*

# Bitter

Where does that bitter tongue come from?
The things that you say are so far wrong,
I remember that sweet little child,
What made you become so wild?

You didn't endure the things that I did,
Yet your love for me you seem to forbid,
I tried my best never to moan,
But all you do is continue to groan.

Throughout my life everyone said, "Jump!"
I did just that, but I took the hump,
I've learned now how to say no,
But that made it worse, now I'm just low.

Is it because I don't have the same father?
If it is then what does that matter?
I've made no difference towards you at all,
But you continue to make me crawl.

No more will I wait for your love or approval,
I'll cut you off, I don't mind the removal,
I've come to terms with your deceit,
Now I'll sit back and take my seat.

# Lost Without My Child

Eight years we spent together not all of them were great,
The love I had for you often turned to hate,
I didn't like to feel that way, but what was I to do?
No matter how I tried there was no changing you.

You had a problem that you would not admit,
Often, at times, making me want to quit,
And in the end it got so bad all we did was split.

You took our child and refused to give her back,
It sent me on a downward spiral and I had to see a quack,
I ended up very ill, strength was what I lacked.

Four years went by and still my heart ached,
I cried most nights, my child was almost eight,
Then I got to see her but after much debate.

Soon you met someone new to help you with our child,
She was quite a bit younger and looked a little wild,
I suppose you thought you had struck gold,
When she looked at you and smiled.

For many years I was lost without my child,
And after such a long wait we are reconciled,
Now we are together stronger and more,
Never will you take her, not like before.

# Friendship

I remember the first day that we became friends,
A friendship I thought that would never end,
So many memories of when we were young,
We did so much together, we had such fun,
We both met our partners and moved away,
No longer in touch every day.

Then we had our children, a blessed day that was,
And our friendship we put on pause,
Some years later you needed my help,
I asked what was wrong, you let out a yelp,
You said that she left you for someone new,
When you told me the story it may me blue.

It brought us closer; I felt your pain,
You thought by this you had something to gain,
You thought our closeness might bring her back,
But common sense, I'm afraid, is what you lacked,
I know that you love her and can't bear the loss,
The fact you won't listen is what makes me cross.

Then you said that you fell in love with me,
You must understand that could never be,
You said that you wanted me in your life,
Sorry to remind you I'm someone else's wife,
We started to drift, as I knew we would,
That friendship we had left with our childhood.

# Don't Look Down

Don't look down and frown at me,
When ugliness is all you see.

Take a look, look a little closer,
There is no chip on my shoulder.

Get to know me if you dare,
Forget the rumours, don't compare.

I'm not the person you thought I was,
So put away those nasty claws.

If you need me I'm always there,
I have a heart, I'll always care.

Break my trust or that bond,
Be assured I won't be conned.

Now's your time to get it right,
Look at me I will not fight.

Gentle as the dove,
My heart will always love.

# Penny Caramel

Remember waiting for the sound of the ice cream van,
Ten pence we had, held tightly in the palm of our hand,
A mixture we had, so many sweets,
Chomping away as we played in the streets.

That special sweet we would keep until last,
The ones before we would eat so fast,
That special one, it only cost a penny,
We would not share it not even with Benny.

The penny caramel we called the dainty,
We chewed and chewed ever so saintly,
No words can describe such a wonderful taste,
Not a bite would we waste.

Times have changed, it's only half the size,
Did they think we'd fall for the disguise?
Children now will never know,
How great it was, what a blow.

No longer does it taste as it did,
That longed for taste when I was a kid,
Everything has changed but not for the better,
All those memories I will continue to treasure.

# Room Fourteen

Walking along the hallway that familiar cold feeling,
As the hairs on my arms stood up, was never
that appealing,
The pounding of my heart as I got closer to the door,
I could have heard a pin drop right there on the floor.

Feeling apprehensive as I slowly turned the key
in the lock,
Holding the cold handle while my body turned to a block.
The room was dark and somber, no one stayed in there,
not anymore,
I could feel the presence right through to my pores.

It was an eerie room with those eyes staring
right through me,
The feeling was heavy on my body, I just wanted to flee.
The bathroom was the coldest almost to freezing point,
What was the story behind this rickety old joint?

I played some music so as not to hear the noise,
The mist at the side of my face of a whispering voice.
Something happened in this room, that I was sure,
I didn't want to stay there and have to endure.

Those eyes 'followed' me all through the room,

Such a cold feeling as I held onto that broom.

On leaving that room the door would always slam shut

They didn't want me in there that I knew for sure.

# A Scot's Hogmanay

It's Hogmanay and so the cleaning starts,
The cleaning aids they're all in the cart,
Sleeves rolled up let's start with the windows,
Us kids we won't make any innuendos.

Our mothers say, "It's a Scots' tradition,"
And, trust me, it's such a mission,
Out with the old, in with the new,
An unclean house that just won't do.

They say it's bad luck if they don't follow through,
And that first foot the front door he must come to,
A tall dark male nothing else will do,
For bad luck is sure to pursue.

He must bring in his hand something for luck,
For if he doesn't that would just suck,
Coal, shortbread, salt, or whisky,
Anything else would be too risky.

One minute to twelve, it's almost time.
They sing that song 'Auld Lang Syne'
I hate that song so I run away,
It makes me cry and I feel so grey.

That old tradition is slowly dying out,
A different generation what's that all about?
Our poor old mothers would give us a belt,
Our Scot's tradition no more heartfelt.

# I'm Not Only A Tree

What do you see,
While you're looking at me?
Don't you realise,
I'm not only a tree?

I'm the air that you breathe,
Each and every day,
In the wind and rain,
Just watch me sway.

In autumn,
I'm naked and cold,
But what do you care?
You're not that old.

I've lived a hundred years,
Shedding, many tears,
Through sunshine and rain,
You'll never experience my pain.

From birth I give you air,
Have some compassion,
And let's be fair,
This tree won't go out of fashion.

# Time

I remember as a child,
Wishing I was older,
Not knowing any better,
Thinking I was bolder.

Now I am an adult,
Thinking back in time,
What was I thinking?
In that head of mine.

Now I tell my children,
Don't wish your time away,
Cherish every moment,
You won't get another day.

Time is very precious,
Love with all your might,
Memories are all you'll have,
At the end of your flight.

# A Child's Love

Just turned fifty I sit and wonder,
Listening to rain, listening to thunder,
What have I achieved? I've achieved many things,
The most important what God brings.

He's given me children, the most precious of all,
The one thing I got right, I'll never see them fall,
I've taught them many things from a young age,
So through the years they'll keep turning the page.

I've taught them to love everyone as equal,
So they can carry on and make the sequel,
My children come first, no matter what,
So those who come between us can go to pot.

I've taught them 'no bullying, no racism, no hate',
They will carry that on and continue to create,
Our children are our future of that you can be sure,
Teach them well and they'll never endure.

So teach your children right from wrong,
You'll teach them well if you keep singing that song,
There's pain and suffering in the world today,
They could be the ones to keep it at bay.

# Parents

What do we know, how can we tell?
When you are hurting and all is not well.


Children you see, we are bonded by blood,
From the moment you're, born you're very much loved.


We teach you to walk, we teach you to talk,
Wipe away your tears, taking care of your fears.


We're with you throughout your childhood years,
Even as adults, we take care of those tears.


We feel your pain every step of the way,
Why do you think we won't call it a day?


It doesn't matter how old you are,
We'll love you forever, near or far.


Don't underestimate the things that we know,
We'll continue to caw just like the crow.


The day will come you'll leave the nest,
Always remember to do your best.

Remembering what we taught you,
Because one day you'll have your own crew.

We'll never leave you stranded when you need us there,
That's how you'll know just how much we care.

# Our Home

Our home is always open to you,
If you feel like visiting, please do,
We are not rich, nor are we poor,
Our door is always open of that you can be sure.

So come on in, sit back and relax,
We're not what you think, we too have cracks,
We treat everyone the same, family or not,
You'll always be welcome and never forgot.

# Those Were The Days

Where did those days go?
When we played kick the can,
They were such happy times,
While waiting for the rag man.

Running around, not a care in the world,
Playing skipping ropes feeling so thrilled,
Hide and seek was so much fun,
While the boys played with their guns.

Cowboys and Indians was their thing,
While we played on our swing,
We played shop and built a den,
And the grown-ups they all called us hen.

We played doctors and nurses, what did we know?
In reality we had a crush on those beaux,
We played a game called Chucky,
Sometimes with money if we were lucky.

We would hear that rag man shout, "Any old rags?"
Then we would be running looking for bags,
We'd poke a hole in an old jumper,
Then hear our mum's shout, "I'm going to thump her."

So many games we played back then,
Lots of fresh air while kicking that can,
Now there's technology what a whack,
I think its time we brought it all back.

# Silence

Silence, I hear you say, something you ask for every day,
No children's laughter, no kisses above your brow,
I can't imagine that right now.

No traffic on the road, no honking horns, no one for you to
scorn,
The streets are empty, nobody in sight just a cold
empty night
Silence is what you wanted, right?

Pause for a moment in your silence, what do you hear?
The emptiness of nothing, now that's something to fear,
They say silence is golden, and that may well be true.

The sound of the ocean on a cold quiet night,
Suddenly, everything seems so bright,
In silence there is no light.

*'I wrote this next poem in memory of Paul, who was a friend of my husband, and whom we had both known since our high school days.'*

# Today We Said Goodbye

Today we said goodbye with memories,
There was no dry eye.

A friend to many, loved by all,
That was their *Paul.*

Always a smile never a bad word,
That's why you are so loved.

Time for all that's what you had,
For which we are glad.

You'll be missed now you've gone home,
With God you're not alone.

With fond memories we'll remember you,
A true friend through and through.

*(You Will Never Walk Alone)*

*In Loving Memory of Paul Joseph Howley*
*(15 October 1965 – 06 August 2016)*

*'May You Forever Rest In Eternal Peace'*

# Country Road

The road I travelled so many years ago is now a distant
memory, buried deep below.
The road I loved and miss so much is a picture now that I can
only touch.
Country road take me to that place, I don't want it to become
a haze, where water flows in the river below and those coal
fires with their glow, the warmth in winter when the snow
would fall and bread in the oven, enough for us all.
Oh, how I miss those valleys with hills and trees as far as the
eye can see, where people came together
on special days,
I really don't want that to become a haze.
Cows in the field as I chopped the logs while the smell of the
coal was never blocked, lambing season the sound of the
sheep as they see their little ones carted off
to the jeep,
A country pub was my Saturday joint, meeting with friends,
drink in hand, while listening to the band.
Oh how I miss that band.

Sunday was best, my day of rest, woken to the sound of the birds outside, sat on the coal bunker, those sounds that told me of their hunger.

Sunday dinner in the oven a fine roast and all the trimmings while humming to music which I found therapeutic.

Trees that formed a tunnel when heavy snow lay above it made me feel like I was wrapped inside a glove, that image will remain with me forever.

What I would give to live in the country again, writing books with my fancy pen, would I ever leave this time?

*No, never again*

*'The next two poems I have written for my friends in Palestine a place close to my heart.'*

# They'll Keep On Fighting

The higher you build those walls,
The taller they will become.
The more you take their rights away,
The more determined they will be,
You cannot deny them, you cannot keep,
Them locked away.

You cannot keep those walls up,
For they are living in a coup,
They will keep fighting,
For what is rightfully theirs,
You cannot keep cutting their water,
And taking their people to slaughter.

You must end this occupation,
Free Palestine and Gaza,
Give them back their freedom,
Give them back their land.

Children must feel safe going to school,
They must feel safe walking the streets,
They must have freedom of speech,
And goals that they can reach.

They must be able to fly overseas,
With their friends and families.


Now its time to lay down your guns,
We must come together and be one,
This land is big enough for everyone,
They cannot continue to run,
It's their homeland you must understand,
You do not have the right, we will make a stand.


You must end the occupation,
Free Palestine and Gaza,
Give them back their freedom,
Give them back their land.

# Palestine My Friend

Palestine will fly free once more,
Those war criminals can't keep knocking at your door,
Killing your loved ones and stealing your land,
We are behind you, we'll keep showing our hand.

They cannot keep you behind that wall,
Stay proud continue to stand tall,
For the day will surely come,
When all the people can be one.

When I came to visit your land,
Beauty is what I saw, I saw it firsthand,
I was made to feel so very welcome,
But the other side has caused so much bedlam.

I came home with a heavy heart,
Knowing your lives have been torn apart,
What could I do other than shout?
Telling my people what it was all about.

There is so much beauty I would gladly live there,
But the conflict would be too much to bear,
I'll continue to pray that the fight will cease,
That soon Palestine will have their peace.

*The State of Palestine Always in my heart*

# Memories Still There

Take your seat, pencils out,
Pay attention, or you'll have a clout,
Listen up, get it right,
Or I'll thrash you with all my might,
That screeching noise runs right through me,
As the teachers smiled in glee.

You, my dear, you got it wrong,
Now you tell me you know better,
Well, seven of the best and your parents get a letter.

That loud noise from the bell,
Oh those days were such hell,
Time for lunch, skip the queue,
You'll have a punch,
Mince and potatoes were so tasty,
Caramel cake and custard was not wasted.

White shirt, navy pants, black tennis shoes,
Never any worries, not even a clue,
Running around while the cold made us blue,
You'll carry on until you can jump it,
That wooden horse was the fun bit.

Pack up, time for home, single file, do not run,
But running was part of the fun,
Home we go to a piece of bread caked in jam,
Such a shame we couldn't afford the ham.

No playing, there was homework to be done, then chores,
Oh, what a bore,
A couple of hours is what we got, street lights on sure Made
us yawn.

In our beds, feeling relaxed, cosy and warm,
That was our place, it was our dorm,
Now we are sleeping,
Happy times with all that dreaming.

Up again, same routine, day after day,
All we wanted was to play,
So excited, summer holidays getting closer,
The fun we will have it will be a roaster.

Seven weeks, no more school,
With our friends lots of swimming at the pool,
Caravan holidays with the family,
Now that sure made us happy.

# The World Through A Child's Eyes

Hello world here I am, just a baby in my pram,
Blurry eyes trying to focus,
So many people taking notice.

Hallowed voices I can hear, wondering are they near?
Feeling warmth in my blanket,
My safe place I take for granted.

Feeling hungry, needing changing,
Life is sweet and very neat,
Love is what I feel, it's my parents they are the real deal.

Crawling done, now to walk,
What a struggle trying to talk,
My parents giggle as they see me wiggle.

It's so funny, I have to say, I'm giggling while I sway,
Back and forth, look at me go,
I'm beginning to feel like a pro.

First day at School what a fright,
Leaving my mother no more in sight,
Tears rolling down my face, as I take it, pace by pace.

Aged eleven, feeling scared, tests are coming I know,
Nothing, what will I do?
I can't get any help from you.

Senior school and so many rules,
I guess I'll just have to play it cool,
So many people, time to make new friends.

It's not that easy; too many trends,
So much stress to meet expectations,
Ready to lay those foundations.

College or Uni what will I do?
I may even be offered a few,
Now I must work to make a living.

Babies are coming, this is my time, I'm blooming,
No parents to help, I'm on my own,
Will I manage? I'll put on a stone.

Getting older and feeling the pain, my bones ache,
Having to sit and take a break,
My babies now married with their own life.

Me, I'm just a wife,
Oh, I wish I was that child again wrapped in that blanket, The
one I took for granted.
Feeling warm and secure there was no pain back then,

Life is short, have some fun,
Sit back and enjoy the run.

# Do Not Judge Me

How many times I have said this,
And still you do it, what is it you miss?
Is it envy like they say?
You don't see me day to day.

Look beyond the weakness you see,
I have a heart I will not plea,
My kindness it is real,
But I'm not so easy to peel.

I'll give you one chance,
When you do me a wrong,
To a certain extent,
I'm pretty strong.

False I'm most certainly not,
Keep doing me wrong,
You'll have had your lot,
And I will remain strong.

Don't try to break me down,
Looking at me with your frown,
I'm not better than you,
I don't pretend to wear no crown.

# Lost Soul

For many years I was just a lost soul,
Trying so hard to stay in control,
Try as I might to keep everyone happy,
It didn't work you were all so snappy.

I still kept trying day after day,
Nothing would shift you, you would not sway,
What made you so angry?
Was it because I was the candy?

Never a smile, never a compliment,
You just thought I was incompetent,
If truth be known,
I felt so alone.

Years later, I now look back,
Sorry for you and what you lack,
Determination is what I had,
For that I am surely glad.

# If Only

If only you could see,
There is no difference,
Between you and me.

If only you could see,
We all have a heart,
Don't tear it apart.

If only you could see,
We came from the same seed,
So we can lead.

If only you could see,
We are all loved,
By the one above.

If only you could see,
What lies ahead,
You wouldn't be so misled.

The moral of the story,
Let's all get on,
Let's live in glory.

# A Thousand Words

Every picture has a meaning,
Good or bad,
Paint it until it's gleaming.

Every song tells a story,
Good or bad,
Sing it in full glory.

Every poem plays a part,
Good or bad,
Write it from the heart.

Paint your picture,
Tell us all,
It's sure to make you ten feet tall.

Sing your song,
Sing it well,
You're sure to come out of that shell.

Write your poem,
Tell your story,
Fill it with amore.

*For what is a poem but a hazardous attempt at self-understanding: it is the deepest part of autobiography.'*

~ Robert Penn Warren

# Voices

Those voices you heard inside your head,
Were cries of babies waiting to be heard,
Beneath the earth is where we lay,
All this time from that fateful day.

Discarded like trash not a care in the world,
Cold hearts they had, were we that troubled?
Our mothers heartbroken they were,
The pain they suffered too much to bear.

They said they were unaware,
Now you tell me how is that fair?
Is it enough just to say a prayer,
Our families' hearts they cannot repair.

They turned a blind eye, that you can be sure,
That blind eye they cannot restore,
They should hang their heads in shame,
They all must share the blame.

Where was their faith? Where was their love?
Too soon they sent us to heaven above,

God, did not want it this way,

It was their rules that took us that day.


So now we have been found we ask of you this,

Admit your sins and take us from this darkness,

Let our families heartbreak cease,

Only then will we rest in peace.

*In loving memory of the mothers and children and all who
have suffered. May they rest in peace*

# I Felt Your Pain

Your pain and suffering did not go unnoticed,
Nor the tears that you cried,
That empty feeling and heavy heart,
That those who sinned had torn apart.

Those who survived now living far away,
I pray your family will find you one day,
It will be a struggle and take some time,
So much was done to hide the crime.

To those involved who knew from the start,
Where was the warmth within your heart?
Think of your own child and how blessed you are,
You must pay the price, it went too far.

Those who inflicted so much pain,
Really, what did you think you had to gain?
The vow of silence you have chosen to take,
Will come back to haunt you, make no mistake.

Mothers and children,

Your cries have been heard,

Together with prayers and love,

Justice will come sure enough.

*I have written this poem in thanks to Mary Lawlor for her hard work and dedication in fighting for justice and all who have, and are still, suffering from events at the mother and baby homes. With special thanks to Philomena Lee 'an inspirational woman' and her daughter, Jane, and in memory of Philomena's son Anthony (Michael Hess), 'A Man of Two Nations and Many Talents'.*

# Where Water Flows & Grass Grows

The waves come crashing in the silence of the night,

Not a sound to be heard yet everything so bright,

Bright in the still of the darkness that surrounds me,

so dark that my eyes could see,

Still not so dark, not to me.


The freezing cold water that glistens by night,

Crisp and clear by day I almost envy it that way,

Whilst the grass grows wild and free who cares

Is it only me?

Where water flows and grass grows what secrets lay
within? Only God knows,

We were born crisp and clean, do you know what I mean?


Look at the birds as they fly wild and free look at them
go I wish it were me.

Voices that echo in the distance not aware of their
existence do they even care?

As my mind wonders let me go and leave me be,

you must understand I want to be free,

Like the birds in the trees while the wind blows,

you don't understand nobody knows.

# Protected By An Angel, Surrounded By Love

A year has passed since that sad day,

When the one we loved was taken away,

'Far too soon,' was everyone's cry,

The grief was seen in every eye.


We were left with tears and sorrow,

And the constant thought,

There would be no tomorrow.


We miss you, Paul,

And always will,

You're loving smile is with us still.


You left a gap that no one could fill,

When you tried to climb,

'That impossible hill'


Our hearts ache for you,

And your very presence,

We feel you all around us,

Our family bonds,

Are of the essence.


Watch over us, Paul,

And you will see,

That in our hearts,

You will always be.


Good Night My Darling Boy,

Love You Forever,

Rest In Peace.


*Written by Elizabeth Howley in memory of her beloved son*
*Paul Joseph Howley*
*15.10.1965 – 06.08.2016*

# Poppies In Heaven

A sea of poppies as they remember the fallen,
who risked their lives,
Not only their lives but their families and, yes,
even their wives,
With hearts in their mouth with every knock on the door,
Worried their loved ones had gone down on the floor.

Guns going off in the fields whilst they hid behind their
shields,
Hearts pounding wondering if this was their time.
Fear in their eyes as loud as their cries,
How could we have known what it was really like?
We can only imagine the pain, suffering and sorrow,
Wondering will they even see tomorrow?

We weren't there, the pain was too much to bear,
Children losing their fathers and mothers too,
This generation don't know, do you?
In countries far away not knowing if they would see
another day,

Writing home in the hope it would get there,

And sometimes not, they couldn't share nor dare tell,

Because the worry caused would be hell.


Some came home and some did not,

When the war ended those who did were left to rot,

Some had no memory it destroyed their soul,

The pain and suffering never to be told.

They were left with nothing except one thing,

Poppies in heaven for those home, they could not bring.

# Justice

Every day we wake up,
Knowing you are gone,
Reality keeps forcing us,
We are feeling so alone.

For those who took your life,
We're sure for no worthy cause,
Are we wrong in hoping,
For justice for our loss?

You left behind family,
Friends and then some,
Aching hearts is what we suffer,
Until our day will come.

No matter how hard we cry or pray,
We know you won't be home,
Knowing that in God's Hands,
You'll never be alone.

When we go to bed at night,
Tears are often shed,

What if's and what for's
Running through our head.

Know that you are loved by all,
Family, friends and more,
And that justice will come,
If it means we'll fight forever more.

*In memory of Andrew Jones (Liverpool)*
*Sadly taken much too soon.*

# Sweet Child Of Mine

Those little faces I held in my hands,
Looking at you feeling so grand,
Those chubby cheeks and dimples too,
That's what I saw while looking at you.

As children go you are three of the best,
Never a dull moment, no time to rest,
Running around day after day,
I wouldn't have it any other way.

Three beautiful daughters that's what I have,
Always smiling always a laugh,
The best dressed around the town,
Really, you should have been wearing a crown.

Beautiful young ladies you've turned out to be,
Look at me I'm full of glee,
And not one time would I stall,
Nothing would I change, I have it all.

*For my precious daughters, Sherri, Chantelle and Sinead*

# Together We Stand

The pain and suffering does not go unnoticed,

Nor the tears that we cry across this land,

A border may separate us but together we stand.


Heavy hearts and tears around the world,

What did they think, we would break and fall?

Not us, we will continue to stand tall.


The more they fight us the stronger we become,

Side by side, near or far, we are but one,

They might as well give up the fight,

Our love for life we do not take light.


We will never be silenced, they will not bring us down,

We don't fight evil with evil, we fight it with love,

That we were given by God above.


London, Manchester, *7/7, 9/11*

It made us stronger and gain more respect,

Our love, our life will not be wrecked.


*(In memory of all who have lost their lives and suffered during*
*terror attacks)*

# Grandmother

I wasn't born when God took you home,
So why do I feel so alone?
I know that you are with me, I have been told,
They say that you love me, so that I will hold.

Forty-two it was no age,
I can't bring myself to turn the page,
I've heard all the stories, they make me smile,
I think you and I would have been top of the pile.

Thick as thieves that's what we would have been,
I would have looked up to you,
Like you were the queen.

One stern look from your eyes,
Would have been enough to make me cry,
But that wouldn't have lasted long,
Because your love would have been so strong.

As I sit here now and think of you,
I often wonder what we would do,
I know you love me through and through.

*In loving memory of my grandmother*
*Ann Jane Johnston McKinlay*
*RIP*
*30 DEC 1913 - 10 SEPT 1957*

# Nobody's Child

I remember the day they took me away,
Going to aunt and uncle's,
That's what they would say,
Three years old, just a child,
That was me, if only they could see.

They could not see the fear in my eyes,
Taken from Mommy with their lies,
Dressed in black it scared me so,
Only Mommy could see it, she did know.

It broke her heart, as it did mine,
What they did was such a crime,
No consent they did not care,
The paper trail, it was not there.

Growing up I tried to find,
The Mommy I left behind,
When I found her, it was too late,
My mind was left in such a state.

Gone to her grave is all they would say,

Not knowing my daddy either that day,

The papers they had not filed,

Now look at me, I'm nobody's child.

*Dedicated to all children taken from their mothers in the mother and baby home era.*

# The Autumnal Tree

Autumn is now upon us,
And the leaves upon the trees,
Are springing into life,
With spectacular beauty,
And masterpiece leaves.

The colours are a pallet,
Of yellow, orange, red and green,
The most beautiful season,
Your eyes have ever seen.

So take a walk and marvel,
At the beauty that's around,
Look up to the trees,
Don't look down to the ground.

The beauty will inspire you,
As there can never be,
Nothing more spectacular,
Than an Autumnal tree.

*Written by Shirley Farr*

# Simple Pleasures

There are simple pleasures in life if only you knew,

How to enjoy them and not feel blue,

What is it that makes you feel good?

Is it art, music or the two?


Perhaps it's poetry that does it for you,

Sit down a minute, just take a pew,

Tell a story, I could tell a few.


You see life is not all bad,

There are those worse off than you,

No food, no water, no home,

To name but a few.


So next time you are feeling blue,

Think of those less fortunate than you,

They have nothing,

If only you knew.

# Dogs

What would I do without my Dawson and Rosie?
Such pleasure they give me, more than a posy,
Two simple dogs but not to me,
Running around wild and free.

I love my dogs, Lhasa Apso they are,
They easily outrun me by far,
So intelligent and fun to watch,
Oh, those dogs are top notch.

Now I am of a certain age,
And no more children can I have,
Dawson and Rosie in my life,
Oh, I get such a laugh.

The time was right to bring them home,
I love to tease them with a bone,
Many years I waited for this day,
Happiness fills me all the way.

# Children

Children, children everywhere,

Listen to me if you dare,

Life is short so make the best,

Of all you have and all the rest.


Cherish the years you have in school,

Do your best to follow the rule,

There is plenty of time for adulthood,

Is that understood?


There is so much in life you can achieve,

All you have to do is believe,

Love yourself and those around,

Stay away from trouble don't end up on the ground.


Try to understand and show compassion,

To those around you when they're not in fashion,

Everyone is equal with unique quality,

Do your best and show your loyalty.

When you're older and looking back,
You'll teach your children what you lacked,
The advice you took when looking back,
Will make you proud and you'll be glad

# A Twig

Imagine a tree that stands before you you're looking at the leaves as they lay on the path, then you look at the shape of that tree and, all of a sudden, you see more clearly. You see, you have the tree, then the branch and, of course, the twig that is barely attached to that branch you then realise that you're that twig and for many years you have hung on to that branch in the hope that, one day, you will grow into a branch which, in turn, makes you feel part of the tree, the family tree.

Suddenly, you begin to feel angry for all those years you missed out on the beautiful colours on each and every leaf, why you ask yourself?

Then, after many more years, you still wait in the hope that your question will be answered, all those leaves that fall become close to the leaves from all the other trees who are related to your tree and who are friends with other trees, but not you, you're just a twig with no leaves, clinging to that branch still hoping, still praying that one day the tree will pull you closer to the branch but it never does.

Those family and friendly leaves who look down on you, they lay on you like you are nothing, but you continue to be proud and strong, but you still ask yourself am I so bad? Is there something wrong with me for wanting to be part of my family tree and to all those related to that tree, including friends?

Deep down everyone treats you the same so you start to question your sanity and wonder is it you? It must be you, right? Because you are nothing more than a twig, crisp and fresh who will continue to be strong, but that makes you different, right?

No, it does not, so you continue to be you. Why would you want to change to please those who are less confident.

Because their leaves are of a slight murky colour? It still hurts I hear you say, well, sadly, it will hurt, it will hurt all your days until the day may come that you, the twig, are brought further into the tree and become a branch, then one day that tree will pull you further again and you gain your leaves and approval which, in turn, will eventually make you one big happy family tree. Then remembering those fallen leaves and the change in colour it makes you think why do they change colour? The answer is simply this, every now and then that change has to come because not one leave is perfect. So, therefore, remember while they poke the eye in your twig, they have a log right there in their own branch.

*'Why do you look at the speck of sawdust in your brother's eye and pay no attention to the plank in your own eye'.*

~ Mathew 7:3-5

# Just A Thought

Never in my wildest dreams did I think I would be where I am today. So much has happened over the years, some good, some not so good and some pretty much ridiculous, but that's life I guess.

Like many, I have seen the T-shirt, bought the T-shirt worn the T-shirt and, in the end, I binned that baggy, raggedy old thing. I've done the first boyfriend and the jealousy bit, I've done the engagement, in fact, three times and I've done the marriage bit twice and, thankfully, the second time I got it right, 'I am so glad I didn't take that job overseas.'

Do I have any regrets? Of course, I don't I think, deep down, any of us do even if we say we do.

People say, 'I wouldn't have done that again,' when, in fact, no, we would have because if we hadn't we wouldn't be where we are today.

And, let's face it, our path is sent to try us, we make mistakes so that we can learn by them, have I? Yes, I sure have.

If someone asked me, 'Would you change anything about your life?' I would say no, I wouldn't, because I have learned, but I would say if I could change a particular situation then, yes, I would and there are quite a few.

I don't regret starting to write so late in life and, no, I'm not going to tell you how old I am (with a wink). Actually, I'm in my early fifties but, trust me, I look in my forties.

I always wanted to write but sometimes life is too fast and the longer we leave it the harder it is, and I'm still learning but most of all I'm enjoying the fact that I'm now in a place of happiness and I'm actually slowing down.

So now I use my spare time to write and anything else that takes my fancy, within reason.

They say it's never too late and they are right, so what are you waiting for? If you have a dream or a passion then get to it as soon as you can, because you don't want to sit back years from now saying, 'What if' or 'if only'.

It's funny actually because, years, ago when I decided I wanted to write I said to myself that my first book would be called 'If Only' but then Geri Halliwell (Spice Girls) brought out her first book and it was called *If Only*. I couldn't believe it and it kind of put me off because, being the airhead I can sometimes be, I thought that I couldn't bring out a book with the same title.

Stupid, I know, and I can hear you saying it by the way (another wink). So here I am doing what I always wanted to do including my website which is still trial and error but it's getting there. As well as that I enjoy photography and taking pictures of the beauty that surrounds us. Back in my school days I took photography but didn't keep it up, I'm not sure why and maybe if I had I may have been a professional by now.

I hated art when I was younger so I didn't care much for artistic pictures, but now it's completely different I love it. As long as a picture tells a story then you have my full attention

I also love sculpture and my favourite sculptor is *Lorenzo Quinn*, son of *Anthony Quinn*, his work is amazing.

Last, but not least, I love anything that involves interior design. My favourite interior designer has to be *Kelly Hoppen,* she has a natural flair for beauty and everything is clean, bright and fresh. The colours she uses and the furnishings complement each other from start to finish, just how I like it.

You will find below an introduction to my next book *Dear Diary* (fiction). Although not a short story this time, more a full length novel due for release in 2018. I just hope I can do it justice.

# A GENTLE SOUL

Never a bad word would pass your lips,
A gentle soul and kind heart,
That was you Moira,
Right from the start.

Back in the day we had such fun,
We grew up then drifted, we had to run,
But never a day would you pass me by,
Time for all, sometimes nay a dry eye.

Remember the punk era the pink hair you adorned,
Perfectly coloured, perfectly toned,
Short black skirt and those holes in your tights,
Never once did I see you fight.

I'm not forgetting 'The Boomtown Rats'
Every song was up there with your stats,
Bob Geldof you loved him so, I'd say,
Aye, Moira go girl go.

Sometimes we'd sing we don't like Monday's
We only like fun days,
Looking back those were fun days,
In reality we lived in a daze.

You've gained your wings,
Its time to say goodnight,
Never will I forget you,
Forever you'll shine bright.
x

*'In loving memory of my dear friend Moira, In Gods arms
you will never be alone'*

# There Are No Tears In Heaven

There are no tears in heaven,
When God welcomes us home,
For there are angels waiting for us,
So we will never be alone.

We did not mean to leave you,
It was not our choice to make,
We were tired in our head,
We were drowning in a lake.

Please try to understand,
The thoughts that were within,
We know that you were close to us,
But they would not let you in.

Depression cannot be cured,
From a medicine cabinet alone,
We need someone to listen, understand and help,
Why can we not get that? We could not deal with the pain
we felt.

There was a story behind our eyes,
That they failed to see,
Depression was good at hiding,
Yes, Even from me.

So please before you go and judge me,
Try to understand the key,
To why it did not fit the lock,
And the pressures that were put on me.

*I have written this poem the way I think those who suffer with mental illness feel, I the hope that there will be more of an understanding and awareness.*

# 'King of the Kop' — 'Brenin y Kop'

The voice you heard from the Kop,
Was no ordinary king of pop,
Dedicated through and through,
That was Jacko, now listen up take a pew.

His dedication to the club,
A devoted fan he was,
Through his voice it could be heard,
And never were there a pause.

Kop - Choir - Gus,
It was no ordinary lust,
The voice of a nation he gave his all,
Never once did he fall.

He traveled far and wide,
Singing loud and full of pride,
His voice could be heard above the rest,
Making him one of Wales finest.

Ian 'Jacko' Roberts,
His blood was Red and White,
Singing loud for his club,
Yes, from the heart with all his might.

A lifelong supporter he always was,
Many a story he could tell,
Singing his rendition of 'Wrexham Lager'
And never did he falter.

Now its time to say goodbye,
Many of us ask ourselves why?
God you see needs him,
A lead angel in the sky.

So overtime you hear,
'Land Of My Fathers'
Thin of Ian 'Jacko' Roberts,
And the friendships that he gathered.

For he will be looking down on you,
On each and every game,
Singing at the top of his voice,
You won't forget his name.

*In loving memory of Ian 'Jacko' Roberts (A fighter until the end) May you forever rest in peace in the arms of God.*

# A Cry For Help

I did not choose to go home so soon,
Listen up I was tuned to the moon,
I did not ask to be depressed,
It's an illness no less.

It could be finances, it could be love or death,
it really doesn't matter, it's a form of grief non the less,
People deal with grief in all sorts of ways,
My mind, it was in a different place.

I cried out for help from those that should have helped,
But instead they plied me with pills,
They didn't tell me the side effects would make me ill.

Those pills they gave me,
They said would make me better,
I followed the instructions right to the letter.

Everything was cloudy each and every day,
Those pill they gave me made it that way,
I couldn't think straight nor for myself,
There I was left on the shelf.

My cries for help went unnoticed,
You did't listen, you didn't focus,
Time and money was your excuse,
You may as well have held the noose.


Deaths by suicide are increasing by the year in the UK alone there are between 10.8 to 10.9 per 100,000 people.

Why?

Because right now here in the *21st* century there is a huge lack of resources not to mention lack of before, during and after care which should be a priority.

It's not only the NHS that are failing us it's the Government and the pharmaceutical companies who make a huge profit on the back of patient illness.

It's a postcode lottery and we now it, we need to fight tooth and nail for the Government to change their policies in regard to patient treatment.

Cancer and Mental Illness are just two of the diseases that should be on top of their list in regard to treatment and cure.

*'These are my thoughts and in my own words'*

# LOVE IS LOVE

Feelings are a wonderful thing,
Not controlled by God,
Nor any living thing.

Who are you to judge?
When you look at me with such disgust,
Have you ever been in love?

The hate in your eyes is clear to see,
Every time you look at me,
Afraid of the unknown is what I see.

When I tell you that I am gay,
Your mind, It starts to sway,
Please don't picture it that way.

Think of love and the happiness it brings,
The warmth of love to all things,
To you, to me, to everybody.

Do not look down at me,
Nor think that I am odd,
The love I feel won't be judged by God.

He gave me life filled with love,
He gave me life to be loved,
Love is Love.

*In support of LGBT*

# Letter To My Dad

Iv'e written a letter to my dad,
His address is heaven above,
There are no stairs to his door,
For me to climb and give him love.

I told him in my letter,
I wish I'd have known him so,
In all the years he was absent,
There was no place for me to go.

I told him about my husband,
Children and grandchildren too,
And wished that he was here with me,
To share the bond and glow.

I told him all about my life,
And all that I have achieved,
I know that he would be proud of me,
Because happiness is the key.

I asked God to look after him,
Until the day I gain my wings,
So I can be with him,
And together we can sing.

So Dad look down on me,
And let me know you are there,
So I can feel you hug me,
And know how much you care.

# A Winters Poem

The wind outside is howling,
The fog is saying low,
The rain is falling heavy,
I think it's going to snow.

There's darkness outside the window,
The moon is shining bright,
I can see the shadows lurking,
With just a flicker of the light.

The frost is slowly gathering,
On the footpath outside the door,
Shiny little diamonds,
That glisten forever more

# Distant Memory

A never ending road,
Driving through the glen,
Wondering why you're taking me,
Down this path again.

A heart that ached so long again
The tears were in full flow,
Why take me back there,
You knew I had to go.

Those old familiar places,
That frequented my life,
Are now a distant memory,
And some of the faces.

# Authors Favourite Quotes:

'*I have already lost touch with a couple of people I used to be*'
~ Joan Didion.
On, Keeping A Notebook

'*Life changes in the instant. The ordinary instant*'

~ Joan Didion,
The Year of Magical Thinking

'*Everybody is a genius. But if you judge a fish by its ability to climb a tree, it will live its whole life believing that it is stupid*'

~ Albert Einstein

'*Its none of their business that you have to learn to write. Let them think you were born that way*'

~ Ernest Hemingway

'*You can, you should, and if your brave enough to start, you will*'

~ Stephen King
On Writing, A Memoir of the Craft

# Acknowledgements

There are so many people I need to acknowledge first I would like to thank *Kim Kimber* (www.kimkimber.co.uk), for copy-editing both *Tears On My Pillow & Where Water Flows And Grass Grows* (poetry) *Sad, Lonely & A Long Way from Home, Secrets & Lies* both (Non-Fiction) and *The Empty Swing* (Fiction)

I would like to thank my friend *Mary Lawlor*, as without her friendship I would never had known about the mother and baby homes both in *Tuam, Galway,* and *Sean Ross Abbey, Roscrea Co Tipperary* where I had the pleasure of meeting some remarkable people including *Philomela Lee* and her daughter *Jane*.

My biggest thanks has to go to my husband, *Jerry*, who continues to support me in my writing and for believing in me. To my Daughters & Grandchildren just for being you, without you all I would not have had the inspiration to achieve the things I have today.

# About The Author

Belinda Conniss is an author and novelist who has published two autobiographical books and two books of poetry, this being a collection of her poetry to date.

Her first fiction title *The Empty Swing*, the first of many short stories.

She regularly blogs about celebrities, events, food, travel and much more.

In her spare time, Belinda enjoys theatre, writes articles on many subjects, promotes many individuals and enjoys photography. You will find Belinda on Twitter and on Facebook:

Belinda's books are available, from www.amazon.co.uk, www.amazon.com and many Amazon online shop's around the globe both in print and on Kindle.

# Coming in 2018

*'Dear Diary'*

Living in Los Angeles wasn't all it was cracked up to be, in fact I would say it was pretty dire most of the time.

Being married to Hollywood's biggest actor and highest paid earner did give me the finer things in life, but what it didn't give me was what most women desired, love.

Sure a lot of woman wanted the expensive clothes, the beautiful homes, the smart cars and all that came with the Hollywood way of life but most were pretty darn miserable.

My life was no different. The only solitude I would get was disappearing to the Hollywood hills to write in my diary about what a miserable existence I had.

Keeping my husband's secrets had proven to be my downfall, and Hollywood's biggest scandal, if it came to light, would bring Hollywood, and many of its income providers, to their knees.

There was a price to pay for living such a lavish lifestyle, and boy did I pay that price! Even my parents came to have a love/hate relationship with me, but who could blame them?

If my father hadn't been a lawyer they would have lost everything. However, they did lose me to a web of lies and deceit, the very thing they taught me never to get caught up in.

## Other Titles by this Author:

*Sad, Lonely & A Long Way From Home*
*Secrets & Lies*
*Tears On My Pillow*
*The Empty Swing*
*Where Water Flows & Grass Grows*

www.insideoutlastyle.com

29322543R00094

Printed in Great Britain
by Amazon